Contents

Games and puzzles

Games and puzzles are good
to play with when it rains.

You have to fit all the shapes in the right place to finish this puzzle. Can you see what the shapes are?

Potato prints

Can you make a painting using potatoes?

What colour paints can you see here?

squish

squish

wooden bricks

8

plastic bricks

Can you guess what
this boy is building?

9

Pitter Patter

Cars and trains

Some cars can go very *FAST* down a ramp.

beep beep

12

An electric train can go really fast, round and round the track.

Dens

It is fun to make your own den when it is wet outside.

What would you use to make a den?

Toy animals

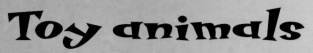

Which animals would you like to play with on a rainy day?

Making cakes

Cakes can be good to make when it rains.

You might need some help making them and eating them!

Rockets

Can you make a rocket out of a cardboard box?

Where will you pretend to go in it?

whoosh!

Actions

painting

building

reading

making

23

Index

The end

Notes for adults

This series supports the young child's knowledge and understanding of their world. The following Early Learning Goals are relevant to the series.
• Find out about, and identify, some features of living things, objects and events that they observe.
• Exploration and investigation: feeling textures and materials.

The series explores a range of different play experiences by looking at features of different toys and the materials they are made from. **Rainy Days** includes things made from the following materials: cardboard, paper, wood, plastic, metal, fabric, glass, and porcelain. Some of the experiences featured in this book include being in a limited space, and playing both alone and with a partner.

There is an opportunity for the child to compare and contrast different toys as well as relating them to their own experiences. Many of the play experiences may be familiar to the child but others will provide the opportunity to talk about and perhaps try new ones.

Follow-up activities
By making direct reference to the book the child can be encouraged to try new experiences such as the following: making cakes, doing a jigsaw, making a den. Taking photographs of the activities would be an excellent way for the child to start making their own book.